IN THE PARTICULAR PARTICULAR

STEPHANIE ANDERSON

IN THE PARTICULAR PARTICULAR

STEPHANIE ANDERSON

NEW MICHIGAN PRESS
Grand Rapids, Michigan

NEW MICHIGAN PRESS
648 CRESCENT NE
GRAND RAPIDS, MI 49503

<http://newmichiganpress.com/nmp>

Orders and queries to nmp@thediagram.com.

ISBN 978-0-9791501-1-1. FIRST PRINTING.

Printed in the United States of America.

Design by Ander Monson.

Cover photos courtesy Anderson Family Archives.

Other acknowledgments in back.

CONTENTS

For KAA & SEA
(DNA)

I.

MISS DORA, HOW ARE THESE FOR APPLES?

Send me back to common school.
My cup is near-brim; from the tucks

I hear you petticoated ones throwing
fits. I can't preserve and never bleach.

Even worse: watts or volts, gulch or gully.
Every year the breach waxes. It's no

temperate thing, this taking. Old eagle
eyes, teach me mending. Tell me writhing.

It's my turn for callus. Tussle and muster
me to ore—my knuckles too glib and my speech

too fainted—facing lady, specter, plain list
of blue squash, task and drive.

WINTER SLAUGHTER

My omnivore, we will eat all but
squeal. I brought you home head-first
in sack, sight-weak one. You barged

scrap-fed with acorn and milk.
Grew long in your board slab
pen. I was glad you could not

see the gun as I sharpened the sticking
knives, skinning knives. In February—
crushing rosin under brick and iron.

We boil water over tires; tub-cradle you
and rub with chains. Hand scrape your nooks,
gaff the hoofs, work in the lime.

At last, you hang burnished and clean.
When I go to fill signal lanterns, I will pocket
you paper-wrapped and larded.

ATONIA

I know how to wake again and again
to the unyielding pear tree. Years ago,
I dozed on a heavy book of dinosaurs.
They grazed by the springhouse,
the stegosaurus saddled ready; startled
by a creak of the stairs, I collapsed
my sheet-tent, fumbled the flashlight
and found the pencil stuck in my palm.

The graphite shadow skulks under
the skin. We're no longer certain who
stitched all these afghans, who stoked
the coal furnace. I think I'll recall.
A few of us sleep still under flour-sack
slips in the tarpaper house, where
the pear tree lazes and through its branches
the night sky descends: sheer as ever.

THE FIRST WAS SAW-SONG

That beacon abandoned in a bucket,
that vestibule-boom. Before Orion

began to hunt overhead, I curled the quizzing
into treads of lore-scape and lunged

for flatlander status like a water
bug's refraction. Screened-in perhaps

and clawing for photons? Tell me,
what does one know of the dense

aperture prior to plunge: an elbow-
print in tar? A swarm? Angles could

unmoor. The last train has always
no caboose. Always, the tune said,

Zero is coming, and is already here.

RAG DOLL WORK

Diurnity, you damn heckler. You grab
my tendons and double-up, jointly.

All day in this box or that Spanish
web—enterology, especially,
requires you. I try to befriend:

snake oil the flex, knot the limbs.
Yet you refuse Adductor muscles

their due. Please, give me back
my dislocation and hairpin; settle
to flexors. During acts my shoulderings

are slip, don't sate the crowd; needle-scale,
weak. Even sleep is not lax without you.

LETTER FROM INSOMNIACS

Loveliest mental placebo
what we have contemplated following:
snake charming, trout tickling,
chicken hypnotism. And not

a single one relieved us, even
post-removal of teeth. Dulled
baskets; water galvanized; that
we sift and gather bulbs

even with the oscillating finger.
Sternum stroke and chalk line method,
mongooses still clustered near

the camp. They nip our
bathrobes as we pace burbling.
Secrecies atilt, us tripping each other.

CARILLON

Come boxcar us, we're foundry-
bound. Brother, it is time and we

be lathed. Haven't I read that
the self is not a fixed sphere?

There are layers involved. Brother,
there are shavings discarded:

metal threaded. Thinned until
curved, you will ring lower

than I, brother mine, in the hanging
open air. We decide our recasting

recast. Not cracked nor welded,
fix but fixed. Take solder,

take hardening; still now.
Then resound, sound, sound.

AT CARRYING LAMPS HELPFULLY THROUGH THE DARKNESS

My green sickness makes the spectators mad;
        all the engines. Tempest suddenly.

        Black eyes best. Pretty knots now
retrograde, now in apogee. Prick-louse tailors—

or fowl, muscatel, or malmsey. But no: a cure?
        Boring of the head, amply dilated

        with aloes. Chess-play censured.
Take brimstone and bitumen, thus, myrrh.

The fumitory purgeth. And foolish
        urbanity, magicians (how they cause,

        how they cure); crocodiles are often jealous.
Proceed with terriculaments, hellebore.

CORYDON PENNSYLVANIA, 1846–1965

I see you've arrived to appraise the latitude
of our light box. Well, sir, we've dove-tailed

planks for want of nails. When the stagecoach
comes from Steamburg, we load the handles

from our factory. Grist, too. Miss Marsh
meanders daily by the river, gathering cattails

and arbutus, thistles and lady slippers. She presents
her bittersweet willows to the Good Templars

and Odd Fellows, murmuring, *Typical name*
for an enamored rustic. You would like to know

the perimeters? Well, lampposts indicate
the half-way mark. And here's Mr. Tome who feeds

the wolf-hunters at the Griffen Hotel. Myself? I look
after the river-ice and arrange the annual ox roast.

Drink where? Why, the distillery up the way.
The road is even—please put away the level.

Is that a measure-tape on your hip? I assure you
the accommodations are most ample. We've set aside

the twin extra-long. You shall dine on hare
and the Aker spinster's rhubarb crisp.

Morrow we'll go to Woodbeck Grove. There's red
maple, mostly, but also mallow and goosegrass.

It's narrow, picking-hour. Berries unacidify
the crisp but one must carry both handsaw

and shears still yes, you see no urgency in our
show. Your eyes betray dam-lust, kind visitor.

II.

ORANGE REFUGIUM

Qualmish? You, who know my want
for groundless, deny this clear-cold?

Below, the tuck and tremble of blue
backcloth and our pinprick shadow

not a provision. We've maxed out
the odometer. Your lips turned

somewhere over Yukon turbulence.
You've begun to question my north-

scape, which seemed like the natural
direction. Let me leap. You can't hear

teeming ahead, the unsnowed plain.
Let me tumble. How it will be alight

with silphium and greensward. I will
guide you down to nearness. To grove.

MOTIVE POWER FOR THE ALTOS

There is two or one subjects.
She knows point-pricks veining
a far bank and benches; not to leave

the train inside a tunnel or on
bridge. (One risks a cloud
of bats.) Her digital bones amiss

the membranes rosy. She's not
beguiled by half-ballast roadbeds
or the chronic destinations.

She knows chromatics work:
activating lights, bent once, snapped
shake. Arrival never activates.

LETTER FROM INSOMNIACS

See last week's salutation. Hail
clobbered mortise and tenon.
There we cram rinds; will skirt
the house with hay.

We're reading your rags. Pardon
intrusions—we find you scrunched
if not reticent. Mimicry attempted
and where did you secrete

instruments? We intend to spend
dead hours in that business,
our self-portraits bluish and foreheads

growing long. Out there, do signs still
read fallout? We've found
cluttered rooms under all sincerely.

BIG BANG POLKA

They built ponds for ice and animals. Afternoons, I wade and muck from spillway to creek. Sift the silt: newt, pollywog, peeper, frog. We live on the ridge, a pump in the root cellar and an uphill source. Clay bands trap rain, sky-coarse. We concrete the wooded springs; house the basin and reserve. Deer run east to the road and to the Clarion river west. Amid we harness water, my tiny dams in the beds.

SITUATION IN YELLOW

Hypsography

The girl has skinned
her palms, which troubles
her coordinates especially.
                                        So she takes

to far wander, matches
and buttons in her trouser
pockets. These are her
                                        boundary monuments.

She does not take paper
clips or protractors.
At the limits, northwest
                                        is lighter,

her relief-shading held
in mind like the notion
of encrusted poplars.
                                        Overedge

has stopped being a daily
concern—she no longer
questions neatlines
                                        or gradicules.

She learns how to measure
hachure by tread, distance
by breath. She sees
                                        no one,

collects half-tones for pigments
she will never mix.
She waits for subsidence
                                        in land, in body.

AT CARRYING LAMPS HELPFULLY THROUGH THE DARKNESS

We have hardly passed the pikes—spindle
fired, we repine. Windmills in a man

head, blind of carping at, yet another hornet
nest. I spangle the eyes, those basilisk tents, or

rather a mincing gait; he wears a whole manor.
On his back, forcible engines and a day-net.

It is no sufficient trial. Where are my girdles,
rebatoes, versicolour ribands? They will crack,

collogue as well. Wrought such toys as
posies, purses, even bundles of apish

irritation. I am an inch and scoff.
Headlong: took all the dicteries I could

heroic. Orator in a jealous humour, be not
dizzard or triviant. Laurel not compelled.

TIC-TOC POLKA

Here time, also, is subject to confluence. Every morning I check the Airguide hygrometer and the bronze hand hovers between *dry* and *moist*. Run-off rinses the rock-base, yet there are no great deltas. The melting was a small pond of our own creation. I have always had a great interest in lichen and where they linger. Every year I clear the fieldstones and sometimes there is celebration. We might have spun to music. Yes, celebration, and a first radio. As we dance, we stumble and steady. Narration reserves sight. We peer under the tires, the tarp and see a glint of snow in the silage. Twilight draws close and early. Does it matter? The mountains and even the manure piles are content to erode. When I feed the Herefords, I hear their settling.

LAST EVENING OF THE YEAR

Bathymetric Map

The boy leaves
his jacket backshore.
The river is icy—reddish
mood, shed as bench mark.

The leadline
clenched in his left fist.
He knows the meander;
steers to levee as if

sightless. Sounds
with wrist-flick, listens
for the undertow.
Considers the water

level; tide
low. The boat shifts
as he picks up altimeter,
determines the sea.

In his hand
he begins to hear
the bottom—its ridges
and canyons, every

ripple and twitch
a shade he cannot
really reach; only feel
tugging from below.

LETTER FROM INSOMNIACS

Thank you for sending piano keys.
Packed in clemency, they fit kind
as adorn. What we meant is
that we're glad you've taken board-

hum with you; more that the rafters
leak it. Though who are we to stay?
We learn every hour skewing dead
plants and trim etcetera. Pinblock

crafting slow as ever due to lack
of laminates. Per your request,
we've enclosed our markings:

they scrawl, but should suit wistly.
You'll see we've not cleared just
clustered spruces to demarcate.

BROKEN REED POLKA

A man is hanging (bungee cord) from pant leg. Voyeur, come away now—vulgarity-prone others will unhook. Here a girl buries and unburies mother's ring. She's grown years while you listened to the currants rip and rush. Fill my jar, hop to. Stop fingering the shoe polish, dust-patterned beneath the stair. Look to lie. Presto ahead. Skip-step and I hide you in my sleeve. A boy eats sausage boiling for the dogs. But now they see us. Cohort shadow, we start the splinter-through. Diminuendo the dervish (not dismal). Don't you hear? We must leave some whirl concealed.

III.

TAR LULLABY

You again. We wade this distillation of peat
and bone. I half-expected the gloss to cut more,

as a slick to quill. You palm stones. The surface is tepid.
Others join the undercoat, and I think I hear the rustle

of passenger pigeons. But on the horizon nothing
swoops or wheels. Where is the aviary, I ask.

What ecliptic? Which azimuth? You point westward
and begin to shiver. Around our waists the murk

mirrors, like the rims of many bells. When we will
arrive, your fists grow heavy, full.

INTERVIEW WITH A MILLINER

Penny? Hearing? Went down for some sure-shot—Autoharp?
and came up having vessels hatched. Chiffon. Or cheesecloth. Flutters in

the vestibule. Liking vagaries. How did you furnish? I carried enamel-
topped tables. Was covered in stellar winds, as was the bathroom wall.

Was what? White matter. About optics? I favored mountains how I practiced
shrinking. Anthracite. I finger-quickened fiber. But what causes

flutter? Isolate: sometimes I am not, some too much. Scarves help.
Stitching? Maybe diphthongs. Weaknesses? Temporal bones. Seasonal

commentary? Winter is second-best: I try to unpaper the ceilings. Addendum?
I bar-abandon garments. Bring your lobes. I'll murmur what I haven't.

A GOOD NIGHT'S NIGHTMARE AND A TIN OF SARDINES

Preferably sideshow. Failing that, snowy
light and a bout of fault; chance
for crackling. My unpuffed bangs and more
same-old. Will've confronted, you

say. Located the root hairs. I follow. Movement
is at least itself not verdant. Will have
unclenching, you say. Nevermind scale
or sand, and don't expect figs. Bet on bark-

coating and caverns—you know the type,
the recoveried type. I never wanted
to ask too hard. Those mass, and there's always

chance for swamp. Still, I thought I knew
primed and I didn't. You say yours are
rubber bands? Mine are rubber bands.

AT CARRYING LAMPS HELPFULLY THROUGH THE DARKNESS

A moth gnaws, furrow-faced, taken with a lask
        or looseness. He could have a falconer's

        wages—fifty talents, parasite complaisance.
What digression of air. Sea-onion is hot and dry

in the third noddie. Irksome hours chid as an egg
        and a chestnut; so I offend; tarry out time.

        Did I macerate myself for this? To have spent
the usual number of years in chopping logic, borrowed

hats? Hobgoblins and horse-leeches are soft fellows.
        Peradventure I light upon a cracked.

THE OTHER POLAROIDS

If I open your hand it will be a faucet
or a camouflage. Just so we're clear, light in
the hayloft is light in a hayloft and hanging

meat is a currant-stained map. Flayed is not
thought. Ungarishly a felling. Next some mud
clumping on rubber boots; some edges look

better burned in. A splinter here, a splinter bare.
Only to be expected: the paint horse watch-eyed
and many shots of cows. Everyone asks

about cows. What else? Too trees in all
the mirrors and sewing machines. Not exactly flirty.
We trace for lines unfocused, demanded, and see

no tinsel in the metal shop. Separate landscapes.
Quarters are the silver yolks in yolk-colored pails.

CORYDON PENNSYLVANIA, CIRCA 1986

Sir, though I am one of few who would extend
to you your former formal address, I feel obliged

to say that mornings are generally stiller now.
Which sometimes pleases me. At the start, cold water

washed closer; the township smeared as through
the hemmed view of a moving train. It seemed to pour

for months. I thought my fingers would shrivel
to twigs from tracing drops. I watched backswimmers

and water striders lace the surface. I might admit
I wish you hadn't done it, but I've heard

rift and rupture sound out to startled lift and it eases
one, knowing our petrifacts sludged in. Preserved

only by my watch. I dive—stratums plunging
our bricks and tumbling our slippers. Sunfish now

near the post with even the foliage in deference.
And how my chronicles, once calm, reduced to ripple.

FROM THE NORTHERN LIGHTS TRUCKSTOP AND MOTEL

He strikes the dinger for a room and a hot whisky.
                                        Hours or days ago, he buried
his camera in heather soot and left the polar
                                        fires oxidizing. He still sees
the grimace of ignited trees. If asked *vocation,* he says
                                        yes, yes, I know shade of garlic
on flesh or chill of a roof-cast aerial. When he picks
                                        up the phone, there is only
the tinkling of a music box. His dreams are oblongs.
                                        Waking he scribbles:
All my previous anythings tied to each other.

I. REAPING

Track east from her elder-blossom patch—
the fieldstone midden routed for fill. Native grasses

rustle up from the still; the Belgians shot
then buried by bulldozer. Their joints

had crackled of late. Now it's all clover and trefoil,
wiregrass underfoot. In September, we gambled

with weather and sickle bar mower. Leave it to air,
then tumble with the tedder. Fork it up, hand over

hand on the rail. She'd help in the loft, raking
loose hay on beams. Her skin coated

and stinging from the dumb cascade. And sometimes
she stood, watching as I seeded winter barley.

II. FALLOW

The September seed rustles from east, crackles
under a bulldozer. Air in loft and hand.
I leave late, stand at the fork where the horses

are coated over. The clover helps my joints;
the trefoil my skin. I regard tracks
as beams, all weather and tumble. Still grasses sting.

The fieldstones are buried and blossoms
gambled to dumb. I take some old wire
as sickle and rout the shot by hand.

Now loosen the rail. The mow fills,
then cascades the patch. Native barley forked
to hay as winter tends the midden.

VARIANTS ON BINDING

Miller's knot, bag knot. I could have been
a cut-up. Might collection

turn profession: occasional nisbit, carting
jars of filberts. I never found

the throwing knives. They corroded;
how smoked meat

turns the color of mahogany. Mahogany
is key. To keep without

cold, try eggs in water-glass. To keep
a pork blood from clot, use salt.

A vinegar for duck. Donkeys are good
watch animals but kill calves.

Safely handle mature bulls only by a ring.
Milk for the fining wines; tannins,

restoration. A carboy when you think
of me and fret the scud. I carry

isinglass in my sack. I tie the neck to whip:
opposing grief knot, preventing fray.

NOTES & ACKNOWLEDGMENTS

"Miss Dora, How Are These for Apples" is a variation on "Miss Annie How are these for apples?", a phrase scrawled across the bottom of a postcard now in the photography collection at the Museum of Modern Art.

All three of the poems titled "At Carrying Lamps Helpfully through the Darkness" take their vocabulary from Burton's *The Anatomy of Melancholy*. The title is from F. Scott Fitzgerald's *Tender is the Night*.

The first sentence of "Tic-Toc Polka" is from Eudora Welty's *One Writer's Beginnings*.

"A Good Night's Nightmare and a Tin of Sardines" takes its title from a line in a Beckett short story.

"Situation in Yellow" and "Last Evening of the Year" are the titles of two paintings by Oscar Bluemner.

Grateful acknowledgment is given to the editors of the following journals, in which some of these poems first appeared or are forthcoming: *American Letters & Commentary, Boston Review, Denver Quarterly, DIAGRAM, LIT,* and *Typo.*

Thank you as well to my friends, teachers, and readers—most especially Samuel Amadon, Timothy Donnelly, and Thomas Hummel. And to my family, particularly ELA, CJA, and BRA, for providing material and much more, thank you. Tadeusz Myslowski advised on the cover art. Finally, utmost gratitude to Ander Monson and New Michigan Press.

STEPHANIE ANDERSON was born in Berkeley, California and raised mostly in Pennsylvania. She lived in Chicago for five years and currently teaches in Harlem and East New York.

❦

NEW MICHIGAN PRESS, based in Grand Rapids, Michigan, prints poetry & fiction chapbooks, especially work that transcends traditional genre. Together with DIAGRAM, NMP sponsors a yearly chapbook competition. Stephanie was the winner in 2006.

DIAGRAM, a journal of text, art, and schematic, is published bimonthly at <http://thediagram.com>. Periodic print anthologies are available from the Del Sol Press, or through the NMP online storefront.

❦

COLOPHON

Text is set in a digital version of Jenson, designed by Robert Slimbach in 1996, and based on the work of punchcutter, printer, and publisher Nicolas Jenson.